MW00880439

Little Black Book

Of

Prayers

Short Effective Prayers That Yield Complete Manifestation

———————

Meagan Farrare

Foreword by: Dr. Hayward R. Hamilton

Her Little Black Book of Prayers

Copyright © 2016 by Meagan Farrare

All rights reserved. No part of this book may be reproduced or transmitted in any form or by any means without written permission from the author.

Edited by: M. Taylor-Gibbs: Teacher325@msn.com

Dedication

To my Husband, thank you for being my biggest cheerleader, loving away all the tears, and for telling me quitting was never an option! This is the first of many!

To my baby sister and my daughter, the same mantle of prayer that I have is on both of your lives as well. Greater works will you do!

Cousin, this would not have been possible without your prayers and daily word count text! Who knew that your 21 days of consecration and prayers would birth this!

To my core, your prayers support and unfailing love has made this journey great! Let us continue to go forth and make Women of Purpose and God's Purposed Girls a global ministry

Table of Contents

Prayers for You

Prayers for Your Relationships

Prayers for Abundant Living

Foreword

As we are undoubtedly fully immersed in the season of "information", sources of data are becoming more and more untrustworthy. However, this writ will be recognized as one of the most applicable, prophetically- sound and user-friendly writings of our day.

Jesus selects 12 disciples, gives them a mission and favors them with His mere presence. This was not enough to proficiently complete the task ahead. The mystery of His will has to be "verbally" expressed in a way that the hearer could properly discern spiritually. This transmission of communication is called "Parabolic Expression". It is not a means to reduce the power of the word but rather make it plain for the receiver to understand.

This prose, Her Little Black Book of Prayers, is a guide to prayer and scriptures to support. It bursts with the POSSIBILITIES of deliverance in every area of human existence, coupled with direction in prophetic prayer. Once you have searched this book, you will resolve within that there is not only nothing too hard for God, but also; YOU can do all things through Christ! This present-aged woman of faith and prayer, Meagan Farrare, is on the pulse of tangible intercession and her ability to transmit the mind of God on paper is noteworthy. I urge you to not only repeat the wealth of confessions, declarations and pleas of this book; but in addition, adopt the level of faith that transcends human comprehension. If you have it; God can heal it. If you are encountering it; there is an answer. Before you give up, grab this book. The mouth of God has spoken, and you need this book in your library.

Now begins the GLOBAL impact of this writ.... May your soul be set ablaze with the fire of God!

-Dr. Hayward R. Hamilton
Hayward R. Hamilton Ministries
Senior Leader of Conquering Power Church Ministries Intl

Introduction

The bible states in Proverbs 18:21 Life and death are in the power of your tongue. Many times we don't see the desires of our hearts manifest in our lives because we won't open our mouths and speak them into existence. The bible instructs us to call those things that be not as though they are. This book is not for you to read silently, but to boldly declare s the prayers aloud into the atmosphere.

The winds of life blow at times and they can seem unbearable, unfair, and calamitous. However we must never lose sight of the fact that if God before us, who can stand against us? You want things to change, then we must change the words that we speak and pray! Speak these strategic prayers and watch them yield complete manifestation in your life!

My challenge for you today is from this day forward never allow the enemy or your circumstances to silence you anymore. No matter what it looks like woman of God VICTORY is yours, so DELARE it!

Prayers for You

Anger

Father I rebuke the assignments that are sent to provoke me to sin in my anger. I am in control of my emotions and I am not ruled by anger. Anger does not control my actions, words, or deeds toward others. Father, I thank you that my words are coated with your love. I decree that I always respond with a soft answer, turning away all wraths as your word instructs me to. I declare that I am not hot-tempered and do not stir up strife. Father, I am not quick to be angered or vexed! Father, in the name of Jesus, I rebuke all manners of bitterness, outrage, anger, indignation, resentment, animosity, quarreling, slander and malice from my life. Father, I decree and declare that I am a ready listener, slow to speak and slow to take offense. Father, expose to me the triggers in the form of words and people which cause me to become angered and produce angered speech. Expose my triggers father so that I can uproot and abolish their assignments from over my life. Father, examine my heart and reveal any harbored anger or inability to forgive that has been hidden with time and has not been uprooted. Father, if any of my actions today that are linked to anger of my past, I ask that you forgive me and show me the areas that need to be addressed right now in the name of Jesus. Father, I denounce the spirit of pride and self-righteousness that would deceive me into believing that retaliation is warranted in any situation I encounter. Father God in heaven I give you permission to search my circle of friends, family, and acquaintances to remove those that are easily given to anger, strife and gossip. Father in the name of Jesus I break the curse of anger and rage going back 8 generations through my bloodline. All medical illness such as hypertension and cancer that have affected those in my bloodline because of anger are rebuked in the name of Jesus. No longer will you torment the people in my bloodline with sickness tied to anger and being unable to forgive. Today I rid myself of the feelings of anger and I strap on temperance, meekness, love, joy, and peace.

Peace, power, and a sound mind rule my life!

Scriptures for Anger

Ephesians 4:26-27 ESV Be angry and do not sin; do not let the sun go down on your anger, and give no opportunity to the devil.

Ecclesiastes 7:9 ESV Be not quick in your spirit to become angry, for anger lodges in the bosom of fools. Proverbs 15:1 ESV A soft answer turns away wrath, but a harsh word stirs up anger.

Ephesians 4:31 ESV Let all bitterness and wrath and anger and clamor and slander be put away from you, along with all malice.

Romans 12:9 ESV Do not take revenge, my dear friends, but leave room for God's wrath, for it is written: "It is mine to avenge; I will repay," says the Lord.

Matthew 5:22 ESV But I say to you that everyone who is angry with his brother will be liable to judgment; whoever insults his brother will be liable to the council; and whoever says, 'You fool!' will be liable to the hell of fire.

Forgiveness

Father, today I make a conscious decision to step outside of my emotions and pain, to forgive those I still bear ill will against. Father, as quickly as you remove my sins from me is as quickly as I forgive others. Today I free them so I may be freed. Father, you know the very pain I feel, but I exalt Your plans above my feelings, for they are temporal. You God are eternal. Father, teach me to be very mindful that the people I need to forgive are also humans with flaws and imperfections just like I. Father, I know that vengeance is yours! Father, I will no longer be concerned with the judgment that comes their way. Today I pray that you will have mercy on them like you continue to have mercy on me. Father, let Your unchanging and unfailing love be shed abroad in my heart that I may love others the way you love us as, Your children. I declare and decree that I am kind, tender hearted and quick to forgive. Father, your word says that hatred stirs up strife, but love covers all offenses. I walk in love today and for the rest of my life. Father I am aware that not forgiving your children is a sin, and the wages of sin are death. Father, give me the words to address those that offend or hurt me, teach me to rebuke in love and allow them to repent. Father, in those situations where

I must forgive without receiving an apology or acknowledgment of wrong doing, help me to make the choice to still forgive. Father, you have called me to produce too much in the earth to allow not forgiving to block the paths of purpose, healing, abundance, or destiny. I will obtain all that God has for me and not forgiving will not be a hindrance. I forgive and I love with the love of God at all times.

Scriptures on Forgiveness

Mark 11:25 ESV And whenever you stand praying, forgive, if you have anything against anyone, so that your Father also who is in heaven may forgive you your trespasses.

Matthew 18:21-22 ESV Then Peter came up and said to him, "Lord, how often will my brother sin against me, and I forgive him? As many as seven times?" Jesus said to him, "I do not say to you seven times, but seventy times seven."

John 13:34 ESV A new commandment I give to you, that you love one another: just as I have loved you, you also are to love one another...

Luke 17:3-4 ESV Pay attention to yourselves! If your brother sins, rebuke him, and if he repents, forgive him, and if he sins against you seven times in the day, and turns to you seven times, saying, 'I repent,' you must forgive him.

Romans 12:17 ESV Repay no one evil for evil, but give thought to do what is honorable in the sight of all.

No More Gossip

No More Being a "Gossip Girl"... Father in the name of Jesus I declare Your Lordship over my life. I submit every aspect of my life to you, including my mouth. I decree that the words of my mouth are not filled with lies, deceit, slander, false accusations or assumptions. I forbid any desires of gaining useless information about individuals for the sake of simple access to information. I seal off my ears from the people around me who continue to speak gossip! I will not entertain these conversations and will cause them to cease in the settings of my attendance. Your word declares that if we keep our tongue in subjection it will also keep us out of trouble. I forbid all manners of corrupt communications from flowing from my lips. My tongue does not have permission to speak evil or deceit! Set a watch over my mouth and be the doors of my lips Father! You word declares that life and death are in the power of the tongue. My tongue is that of a ready writer; always edifying and speaking life over individuals and situations. I bind the spirit of retaliation that would deceive me into slandering another one of your children! I will not backbite, gossip, or speak negatively on anyone- familiar or unfamiliar! My tongue is that of a tree of life! Father just as your word declares, I decree that blessings and cursing cannot flow from the same mouth. I will not hinder my blessings by the negative words I speak concerning others! I align myself with the truth of your word so that my life is not defiled by the words that I speak! I avoid quarreling and argumentative conversations that breed self-righteous or prideful behavior! 1 Thessalonians 4:11 is the reality of my life! I mind my own business and tend to the work you have mandated me to complete! I will not be negatively influenced by media such as reality TV, internet sites, music, or social media that produces an atmosphere for gossip! I no longer have an appetite for gossip regarding celebrities or those in my circle! I have an unquenchable appetite to uphold your statues of speaking life and all things true. I think and speak only those things that are pure, holy, and truth bearing. I am your light here on earth, and I will not be viewed as one who tears down Your children! I am an encourager and an up lifter to all those who I encounter! I possess such a persona and anointing that gossipers will not have those conversations in my presence. I have a controlled tongue and gossip is no longer a part of my life.

Scriptures about Gossip

Proverbs 21:23 ESV Whoever keeps his mouth and tongue keeps himself out of trouble.

Ephesians 4:29 ESV Let no corrupting talk come out of your mouths, but only such as is good for building up, as fits the occasion, that it may give grace to those who hear.

Proverbs 15:1 ESV A soft answer turns away wrath, but a harsh word stirs up anger.

Psalm 34:13 ESV Keep your tongue from evil and your lips from speaking deceit.

Psalm 141:3 ESV Set a guard, O LORD, over my mouth; keep watch over the door of my lips!

James 1:26 ESV If anyone thinks he is religious and does not bridle his tongue but deceives his heart, this person's religion is worthless.

Proverbs 18:21 ESV Death and life are in the power of the tongue, and those who love it will eat its fruits.

James 3:10 ESV From the same mouth come blessing and cursing. My brothers, these things ought not to be so.

Titus 3:2 ESV To speak evil of no one, to avoid quarreling, to be gentle, and to show perfect courtesy toward all people

1 Thessalonians 4:11 NIV and to make it your ambition to lead a quiet life: You should mind your own business and work with your hands, just as we told you

Healing of My Past

I decree and declare that I am free from every demonic spirit sent to keep me in the bondage of my past. I boldly declare that today I am free from all past hurts, mishaps and traumatic experiences! I speak to my heart, every hidden and harbored hurt you be exposed in the name of Jesus. What the enemy sent to my life to try and destroy me, God you are working in my favor! I am not the person I used to be. I am not the evidence or result of the things that have happened to me! I am set free from all manners of condemnation, disappointment, shame or guilt! Your word declares that who the Son sets free is free indeed! I was saved by your blood. I am no longer bound by the chains, nor the events of my past. I love my family and friends- even those who abandoned and rejected me! I love them the way you love me! I declare that this day they are released from my inability to forgive. Bitterness and I no longer can coexist. I will not allow my past to live in my present or future! I decree and declare that every vision, dream, or memory that the enemy uses to taunt me with the memories and feelings of my past to cease operation in my mind right now, in the name of Jesus! I cast down every vain thought that is sent with assignment to condemn me. Every traumatic experience of my life was sent to make me stronger and help me deliver another person traveling through the same storm I faced! You have freed me to talk about my past. Speaking on my past no longer brings about ill feelings. Those moments are now only memories created to make me the stronger person who stands before you today. Every anxiety, fear, or doubt that tries to inhabit my mind or alter the new creation you created me to be; their assignments are null and void right now in the name of Jesus. I am not who I once was! I am not who they said I was or was going to be! As far as the east is from that west that is how far God you removed my transgressions from me! When you look at me you don't see the sins of me-you see your Son's precious blood! I declare that I forgive myself just as you have forgiven me! I am no longer ruled by bitterness, resentment, or harbored hurts! I am loving, free, and operating in the purpose you have created for me! My past is my testimony used as a tool to deliver everyone I encounter! Satan had a plot, but you God had a plan! A plan to prosper me and everything that has happened to me is working for my good. I will always maintain my countenance for in this life. I may have experienced tribulation but you have already overcome the world! Greater is he that is in me than he that is in the world! Dear Past, you are behind me, and that is where you shall remain! Behold, this woman is a NEW CREATURE!

Scriptures on Emotional Healing

Romans 8:1 ESV There is therefore now no condemnation for those who are in Christ Jesus.

1 John 3:20 ESV For whenever our heart condemns us, God is greater than our heart, and he knows everything.

Psalm 103:10 ESV He does not deal with us according to our sins, nor repay us according to our iniquities.

2 Corinthians 5:17 ESV Therefore, if anyone is in Christ, he is a new creation. The old has passed away; behold, the new has come.

Romans 8:37-39 ESV No, in all these things we are more than conquerors through him who loved us. For I am sure that neither death nor life, nor angels nor rulers, nor things present nor things to come, nor powers, nor height nor depth, nor anything else in all creation, will be able to separate us from the love of God in Christ Jesus our Lord.

Philippians 4:8 ESV Finally, brothers, whatever is true, whatever is honorable, whatever is just, whatever is pure, whatever is lovely, whatever is commendable, if there is any excellence, if there is anything worthy of praise, think about these things.

Godly Living

Lord I thank you that as I choose the sober decision every day to follow you, you are continuing to perfect all things that concern me. I thank you that as I continue to study Your word and commune with you, my desires for ungodly things and companionship diminish. I thank you Lord that my circle of friends are like minded individuals who motivate me in the very things you have called me to do. I thank you that my outlook on life is being renewed, and that my mind is ever being transformed by Your word. Lord you said that those that are in Christ are a new creature. I thank you that I am a new creature and that old things and desires are passed away. God as I become inundated with your purpose for my life, new God-centered desires, friends, and hobbies are being birthed in me like never before. Father I thank you for allowing me to have constant undeniable experiences with you that help strengthen my ability to stand during this transition of my life. Father, train my mouth to speak in faith concerning the promises of my lips. I forbid a speech of doubt, lack of faith, and unbelief! My tongue is that of a ready writer declaring and decreeing the newness of me and my life in you. Father, teach me to be loving towards your children even in difficult times. Father, I know that there will be resistance when my inner circle of friends and family see the change in me. Father, I thank you for giving me the strength to not be offended and still walk in love with those who don't understand the place you are taking me to. I thank You that no longer will I live under the bondage of Satan's plot for my life, but I now live as a servant of the Lord walking in all humility, gentleness, and patience; bearing one another in love a manner that is worthy of the call you have called me to! Father, as people and things of my former life began to leave, I know that I am never alone for you will never leave nor forsake me.

I love the new me! I love my new hobbies! I love my new found friendship with you Father and your word! Thank you for saving my life. Now I will live my life always edifying and glorifying you in everything that I do!

Scriptures for Godly Living

Romans 12:2 ESV Do not be conformed to this world, but be transformed by the renewal of your mind, that by testing you may discern what is the will of God, what is good and acceptable and perfect.

Ephesians 4:32 ESV Be kind to one another, tenderhearted, forgiving one another, as God in Christ forgave you.

Romans 12:1 ESV I appeal to you therefore, brothers, by the mercies of God, to present your bodies as a living sacrifice, holy and acceptable to God, which is your spiritual worship

Philippians 4:8-9 ESV Finally, brothers, whatever is true, whatever is honorable, whatever is just, whatever is pure, whatever is lovely, whatever is commendable, if there is any excellence, if there is anything worthy of praise, think about these things. What you have learned and received and heard and seen in me—practice these things, and the God of peace will be with you.

1 John 2:15-17 ESV Do not love the world or the things in the world. If anyone loves the world, the love of the Father is not in him. For all that is in the world—the desires of the flesh and the desires of the eyes and

pride in possessions—is not from the Father but is from the world. And the world is passing away along with its desires, but whoever does the will of God abides forever.

Galatians 5:19-21 ESV Now the works of the flesh are evident: sexual immorality, impurity, sensuality, idolatry, sorcery, enmity, strife, jealousy, fits of anger, rivalries, dissensions, divisions, envy, drunkenness, orgies, and things like these. I warn you, as I warned you before, that those who do such things will not inherit the kingdom of God

Confidence

Lord I thank you for making me perfect in your eyes. I marvel at such an awesome Creator you are. I am grateful for all that you created me to be. In the very womb of my mother you formed even the most intricate parts of who I am, I am fearfully and wonderfully made! I refuse to listen to the critique of the world because they don't compare to the excellence you created me in. I love my hair and its texture! I love my eyes and their shape! I love every unique or plain feature of my body! Some may look like me, but I am one of a kind! You broke the mold when you made me God! I can look in the mirror and boldly declare 'Girl you are cut from a different cloth!' I will never look for man's approval for you love me just as I am. Not one mistake was made in my creation. You are the Creator, and because you created them there is no failure or mistakes! I love my lips, breast, hips legs and even my toes! God, you knew EXACTLY what you were doing when you put me here for a purpose! Jesus' blood is the only stamp of approval I need! I am created in the very image of you! My inward appearance is just as beautiful of my outward appearance. I embrace my shape and all the things society frowns upon. You sent your precious Son to die for me! God, that meant to you, I was to die for! The negative views and words that were assigned to be spoken to cause low self-esteem and insecurities are null and void! The words spoken to me by family members as a child, I release them from my heart for they do not define me! You word defines me! I am bold. I am confident. God, I am stunning! I boldly declare that I will never cast away my confidence because in it there is a great reward from you. You uphold me in Your righteous hand. I am a royal crown beauty, a diadem in your hands Lord! When I gave my life over to you I became a new creature. Each and every flaw and insecurity has passed away. I will never slip back into the bondage of fear for I am Daddy's little girl and I call you Abba, Father! My confidence and self-esteem is like a tree planted by the rivers of water. Nothing can alter my belief for myself. Your word declares 'as a man think so is he'! I love what I see! I love my laugh! I love my voice! I love every fiber of my being because I was made perfectly by You! In you there is no failure and you never make any mistakes! I am exactly who You say that I am!

Scriptures for Confidence

Song of Solomon 4:7 ESV You are altogether beautiful, my love; there is no flaw in you.

Psalm 139:13-14 ESV For you formed my inward parts; you knitted me together in my mother's womb. I praise you, for I am fearfully and wonderfully made. Wonderful are your works; my soul knows it very well.

1 Samuel 16:7 ESV But the LORD said to Samuel, "Do not look on his appearance or on the height of his stature, because I have rejected him. For the LORD sees not as man sees: man looks on the outward appearance, but the LORD looks on the heart."

Joshua 1:9 ESV Have I not commanded you? Be strong and courageous. Do not be frightened, and do not be dismayed, for the LORD your God is with you wherever you go."

Genesis 1:27 ESV So God created man in his own image, in the image of God he created him; male and female he created them.

Luke 12:7 ESV Why, even the hairs of your head are all numbered. Fear not; you are of more value than many sparrows
.

Psalm 139:14 ESV I praise you, for I am fearfully and wonderfully made. Wonderful are your works; my soul knows it very well.

Hebrews 10:35 ESV Therefore do not throw away your confidence, which has a great reward.

Isaiah 62:3 ESV You shall be a crown of beauty in the hand of the LORD, and a royal diadem in the hand of your God.

Romans 8:15 ESV For you did not receive the spirit of slavery to fall back into fear, but you have received the Spirit of adoption as sons, by whom we cry, "Abba! Father!"

Addiction

Father God in heaven I place you back on the throne of my life where you belong! I pull down myself, my pride, and my fleshly desires right now and place them under subjection to your word! I decree and declare that the bondage of sin and addiction are broken from over my life right now in the name of Jesus! I repent Father for allowing this addiction to govern and function as the God of my life! You are the only true and living God and the only person who is sovereignly in control of my life. I decree that the appetite of this addiction cease its operation in my life right now in the name of Jesus. I seal my life off from people, places, and things that trigger these fleshy desires to return. Daily I kill my flesh and strap on your holy lifestyle! Alcohol, prescription drugs, illegal drugs, gambling, tobacco, sex, pornography, shopping, and self-inflicted pain such as cutting- your hold is loosed from over my life right now in the name of Jesus! I rise up and take dominion over you by the authority God has given to me. I no longer desire you! I no longer have an appetite for you! I am no longer controlled by you! I am steadfast and unmovable in the things of God. Father replace my addiction to sin with new found unquenchable hunger and thirst for Your presence and communion with your word. In my moments of weakness I will be ever mindful that you have provided a way of escape already. I am hastening to that escape at all times. I can do all things through Christ because my strength comes from you Lord. Your grace is sufficient for me. Your strength is perfect in my moments of weakness. I am an overcomer and I am delivered from the hands of addiction from this moment of declaration forward. Who the Son sets free is free in deed and to day I declare is the first day of the best days of my addiction free life!

Corinthians 10:13 ESV No temptation has overtaken you that is not common to man. God is faithful, and he will not let you be tempted beyond your ability, but with the temptation he will also provide the way of escape, that you may be able to endure it.

Galatians 5:16 ESV But I say, walk by the Spirit, and you will not gratify the desires of the flesh.

James 4:7 ESV Submit yourselves therefore to God. Resist the devil, and he will flee from you.

1 Corinthians 6:18-20 ESV Flee from sexual immorality. Every other sin a person commits is outside the body, but the sexually immoral person sins against his own body. Or do you not know that your body is a temple of the Holy Spirit within you, whom you have from God? You are not your own, for you were bought with a price. So glorify God in your body.

1 John 1:9 ESV If we confess our sins, he is faithful and just to forgive us our sins and to cleanse us from all unrighteousness.

Romans 12:2 ESV Do not be conformed to this world, but be transformed by the renewal of your mind, that by testing you may discern what is the will of God, what is good and acceptable and perfect.

1 John 5:4 ESV For everyone who has been born of God overcomes the world. And this is the victory that has overcome the world—our faith.

1 Corinthians 15:33 ESV Do not be deceived: "Bad company ruins good morals."

Matthew 6:13 ESV And lead us not into temptation, but deliver us from evil.

Depression

Father, these feelings that I feel right now are temporal! You God are eternal! Father I come laying down the burdens that I have tried to carry with my own human abilities. I need you Lord. Your word declares that when the righteous cry for help you hear and deliver them. Your word declares that you stand close to the brokenhearted and saved those with a crushed spirit. I decree and declare feelings of sadness, oppression, anxiety, worry, fear, insecurities, helplessness and reckless behavior must exit my life right now in the name of Jesus. I speak to every traumatic experience of my past and declare that I will no longer be subject to the torment in my mind any longer. Father your word declares that who the Son sets free is free in deed. I am free and refuse to return to operate from oppression or depression ever again. I have joy, peace, confidence, and I am abounding in the rewards of my salvation. I will not lean unto my own understanding any longer! I cast every care over to you at this very moment and I chose to take on your yolk for it is easy and yours is light. Your word declares that I am fearfully and wonderfully made by You. God, You love me with an unfailing love. As I seek help in the natural I will also spend time in praying and declaring that I no longer struggle with depression, that I have victory in my mind. I am not alone for you are with me always. In spite of what it appears to be, you love me right here right now- even in this temporary broken state. You have a future and a hope for me. You are turning my mourning into dancing! Morning is right now and my Joy is here NOW! This weight is being lifted and the King of Glory shall enter into my life like never before. I speak liberation to the bound areas of my mind. I operate from my God-given authority of power, love, and a sound mind. A sound mind belongs to me in Jesus name! I curse these temporary feelings at the root! I will wait on you Lord, for you will renew my strength like the wings of an eagle and I will mount up, run and not be weary, and walk and not faint. You are the lifter of my head! Countenance be lifted right now in the name of Jesus for these present sufferings cannot be compared to the glory that God is revealing in my life. This very hard place is working for my good! I can and I will overcome by the blood of the lamb and the word of my testimony! Depression you are in my past! You are a defeated foe! I am surrounded by a great cloud of witnesses and I lay every weight that is trying to cling to me. I will run with endurance and finish this race of purpose for my life.

Scriptures Defeating Depression

Matthew 11:28 ESV Come to me, all who labor and are heavy laden, and I will give you rest.

1 Peter 5:7 ESV Casting all your anxieties on him, because he cares for you.

Jeremiah 29:11 ESV For I know the plans I have for you, declares the LORD, plans for welfare and not for evil, to give you a future and a hope.

Proverbs 3:5-6 ESV Trust in the LORD with all your heart, and do not lean on your own understanding. In all your ways acknowledge him, and he will make straight your paths.

Psalm 143:7-8 ESV Answer me quickly, O LORD! My spirit fails! Hide not your face from me, lest I be like those who go down to the pit. Let me hear in the morning of your steadfast love, for in you I trust. Make me know the way I should go, for to you I lift up my soul.

Psalm 23:4 ESV Even though I walk through the valley of the shadow of death, I will fear no evil, for you are with me; your rod and your staff, they comfort me.

Philippians 4:6-7 ESV Do not be anxious about anything, but in everything by prayer and supplication with thanksgiving let your requests be made known to God. And the peace of God, which surpasses all understanding, will guard your hearts and your minds in Christ Jesus.

2 Timothy 1:7 ESV For God gave us a spirit not of fear but of power and love and self-control.

Proverbs 12:25 ESV Anxiety in a man's heart weighs him down, but a good word makes him glad

Procrastination

Father I boldly declare that the python spirit of procrastination that has tried to squeeze the life and production of the things you have called me to be is cursed at the root. I evict procrastination from every aspect of my life in Jesus name. Father I decree that just as your word declares my hand is diligent and I will possess, rule, and obtain all the territory that is ordained for me. I bind up every situation sent to distract, deter, or steal my determination or discipline. I seal off my life from laziness and slothfulness in the name of Jesus! I forbid their operations in my life from this day forward! Father I know that the very things you have required of me are right in your eyes and I refuse to live in sin due to a failure to progress! I declare that I am always progressing and never stagnant another day of my life. Daily you are renewing my energy to accomplish the task you have given me! As the word states I can do all things through Christ that strengthens me! I decree that my passion will never die! I speak to every dry bone in my life and declare that it lives in the name of Jesus. I bind up the cyclical cycle of putting off tasks, idleness, non-accomplishment, and underachieving from over the life and purpose you have called forth in the name of

Jesus. I declare that I will birth every assignment you have called me to in the right season, producing on time ripe fruit. I decree and declare that my season of Abram has come to an end, I am now walking in the anointing of Abraham- a father over all that you have called me to. I take my rightful place in purpose right now in the name of Jesus. Your word declares that life and death are in my tongue! Father I boldly confess that from this day forward I am an achiever! I am an overcomer! I am a goal demolisher! I am seizing every opportunity and door You open unto me. I prosper in my business and career, I do not delay that what needs to be accomplished today for tomorrow! Procrastination I boldly declare that you will no longer rob me of purpose and destiny! I will fulfill the assignments and the will of God for my life.

Scriptures against Procrastination

Proverbs 13:4 ESV The soul of the sluggard craves and gets nothing, while the soul of the diligent is richly supplied.

Proverbs 12:24 ESV The hand of the diligent will rule, while the slothful will be put to forced labor.

Proverbs 20:4 ESV The sluggard does not plow in the autumn; he will seek at harvest and have nothing.

Ephesians 5:15-17 ESV look carefully then how you walk, not as unwise but as wise, making the best use of the time, because the days are evil. Therefore do not be foolish, but understand what the will of the Lord is.

Proverbs 27:1 ESV Do not boast about tomorrow, for you do not know what a day may bring.

James 4:17 ESV So whoever knows the right thing to do and fails to do it, for him it is sin.

Luke 12:40 ESV You also must be ready, for the Son of Man is coming at an hour you do not expect."

Hebrews 12:11 ESV For the moment all discipline seems painful rather than pleasant, but later it yields the peaceful fruit of righteousness to those who have been trained by it.

Proverbs 20:13 ESV Love not sleep, lest you come to poverty; open your eyes, and you will have plenty of bread.

Purpose Fulfillment

Father You spoke me into The Earth with a divine assignment to fulfill while I am here. It is my complete desire that when I return back to you that I have not an ounce of talent, gifting, or anointing left. I declare that my life's agenda and desires are totally subject to Your will for my life. I am your partner here on earth. You are committed to fulfill your very heart's desire through me. I am determined, disciplined, and unwavering as I chase my purpose down. I bind every plot, scheme, and strategy that Satan has assigned to get me distracted, complacent, or stagnant and I cast them to very pits of Hell! Greater is He that is in me than He that has risen up against me. I am more than a conqueror. I am possessing the land of my enlarged territory. I am like a tree planted by the rivers of water- steadfast and unmovable in my purpose. I seal off my ears from receiving any word that is contrary to that what you have commanded for me. I will only speak to those whom you give me permission to, and in the season you permit concerning the plan You have for me. I will not cast my pearls before people of doubt, lack of faith, or unbelief. Father those individuals who are assigned to my life to help cultivate and launch me into my purpose, I thank you, that I am coming in contact with them in the divine timing you appointed. I declare that I always operate from a sober and Spirit led countenance. I do not allow myself to make emotional, rushed, or hasty decisions. My moves are strategic, purposeful, and intended by God. My moves are also sound through prayer and discernment. Father, remove the smoke screens from my eyes. Allow my eyes to see the accurate and precise purpose for my life. I harken unto your voice for provision. The voice of a stranger I will not follow! I decree that the atmosphere which is conducive for producing the resources needed to fulfill destiny is coming into alignment with me right now. I decree that my presence is an atmosphere shifter! Every climate I enter will shift in my favor at the very opening of my mouth! I have favor with all those I encounter! Father I stand in faith that you are raising up individuals to sow into your vision for my purpose. Purpose you will be fulfilled all the days of my life!

Scriptures on Purpose Fulfillment

Jeremiah 29:11 ESV For I know the plans I have for you, declares the LORD, plans for welfare and not for evil, to give you a future and a hope

Romans 8:28 ESV And we know that for those who love God all things work together for good, for those who are called according to his purpose.

Psalm 138:8 ESV The LORD will fulfill his purpose for me; your steadfast love, O LORD, endures forever. Do not forsake the work of your hands.

Isaiah 55:11 ESV So shall my word be that goes out from my mouth; it shall not return to me empty, but it shall accomplish that which I purpose, and shall succeed in the thing for which I sent it.

Ephesians 1:4-5 ESV Even as he chose us in him before the foundation of the world, that we should be holy and blameless before him. In love he predestined us for adoption as sons through Jesus Christ, according to the purpose of his will,

Romans 5:3-5 ESV More than that, we rejoice in our sufferings, knowing that suffering produces endurance, and endurance produces character, and character produces hope, and hope does not put us to shame, because God's love has been poured into our hearts through the Holy Spirit who has been given to us.

Healing

Father your word declares that Healing belongs to your children. It is the very inheritance of our salvation and our communion with you. I thank You that regardless of the doctor reports I will never be sick another day in my life. 1 Peter 2:24, Jeremiah 33:6, and Psalm 119:50 are reality for me each and every day of my life. My body functions in the excellence that You have created it to function. My immune system has the ability to ward off, dematerialize, and neutralize any bacterial or viral infections that try to inhabit my body. My blood pressure is that of an acceptable rate of 120/80. My pancreas produces the proper amount of insulin to maintain healthy blood sugar levels. My cholesterol is regulated- all in Jesus' name. I forbid an overactive or underactive thyroid. I decree and declare that my female organs (every last one) are normal. My menstrual cycle is that of a normal woman! I forbid any irregularities in my cycle or sudden increases or decreases in my hormone levels that control my moods. I decree and declare that the blood flows unrestricted through my veins. I forbid any blood clots, pulmonary embolisms, or aneurism. You know the number of the hairs on my head! My fingernails are healthy and strong- not easily damaged. My skin is producing the proper oils and my pores are unclogged, allowing my skin to remain clear and free from breakouts and blemishes. As I mature in age, my ears and eyes continue to function at the same level as that of a young person! My vision is enhancing right now in the name of Jesus! 20/20 vision belongs to me! It is my inheritance. Heart you will beat with the rhythm of life! You are strong healthy and a normal size heart! My gastral and urinary tract are free from blockage, infections, or hindrances. My bone and joints are strong and healthy I forbid any breaks bruises or fractures in the mighty name of Jesus! Migraine, tension, and cluster headaches I command you to cease your operation right now in the name of Jesus. Cancer, AIDS/HIV, Hepatitis and any other blood pathogen diseases I curse you at root and declare and decree that you will never invade my temple! Growths, cyst, benign tumors and cancerous tumors, we curse you at the root! Dry up and dissolve! I declare that the blood supply that is sustaining your existence in my body right to be cut off right now in the name of Jesus! My body is a temple where the Holy Spirit and Jesus abide, therefore sickness and diseases cannot infiltrate my body. Body you will line up right now in the precious name of Jesus! Body you were bought with an eternal price of Jesus' blood! Therefore as the healing virtue of Jesus flows from the crown of my head to the very soles of my feet, my body is lining up and living out the truth that above all else you desire us to prosper and be in health even as our souls prosper. I am healed and will never be sick another day of my life!

Scriptures for Healing

Isaiah 53:5 ESV He was wounded for our transgressions, He was bruised for our iniquities; the chastisement for our peace was upon Him, and by His stripes we are healed.

Matthew 8:17 ESV He Himself took our infirmities and bore our sicknesses.

Proverbs 3:8 ESV It will be health to your flesh, and strength to your bones.

Psalm 118:17 ESV I shall not die, but live, and declare the works of the Lord

3John:2 ESV Beloved, I pray that you may prosper in all things and be in health, just as your soul prospers.

James 5:15 ESV And the prayer of faith will save the sick, and the Lord will raise him up. And if he has committed sins, he will be forgiven.

1Peter 2:24 ESV (Jesus) bore our sins in His own body on the tree, that we, having died to sins, might live for righteousness -- by whose stripes you were healed.

Loneliness

God I thank you for your unchanging and unfailing love. A love that never changes in spite of what I do. God I thank you for being a friend that sticks closer than a brother. You are my comforter, my helper, my confidant, my counselor, and my peace! Just like you met the Samarian Woman at the well...that is the same way you are meeting me in my need for companionship right now. These feelings of loneliness are a lie from the pits of hell! Your word declares that you will never leave me nor forsake me. I have you Lord, and because of that, I am never alone. Father, today examine my heart and every place where I have tried to fill voids of hurt with materialism and human desires. I decree and declare that those places are filled with the love and thirst for Your presence and word. Father increase my appetite to commune and tarry with you. Father let my reading time with you be enhanced so that the logos on the pages become a right now rhema word in my life. Every person that has abandoned me, left me, discouraged me, or told me I didn't fit in; I release and forgive right now! I live a full and satisfied life with you God; a friend that sticks closer than a brother. Before being conceived in my mother's womb Your hand magnificently created me, then declared over my life that I am forever fearfully and wonderfully made. I decree and declare that my life is evidence of just how great the only true and living God is. Just like Jonah in the whale, in the belly of any circumstance you hear my cry, and harken unto my call! I am never alone! For you are with me and thy rod and staff they comfort me. You are nigh to the brokenhearted and save those of a contrite spirit. I cling to you Father on this day like never before! Wrap me in Your arms and hide me in the shadow of Your wings. Every burden is being lifted! Every yolk of bondage is being destroyed. This day my mourning is turning into dancing! Today I dance and rejoice with you Abba, Father, Daddy... GOD!

Scriptures for Loneliness

Isaiah 41:10 ESV Fear not, for I am with you; be not dismayed, for I am your God; I will strengthen you, I will help you, I will uphold you with my righteous right hand.

Joshua 1:5 ESV No man shall be able to stand before you all the days of your life. Just as I was with Moses, so I will be with you. I will not leave you or forsake you.

Psalm 23:4 ESV Even though I walk through the valley of the shadow of death, I will fear no evil, for you are with me; your rod and your staff, they comfort me.

Psalm 27:10 ESV For my father and my mother have forsaken me, but the LORD will take me in.

Isaiah 40:28-31 ESV Have you not known? Have you not heard? The LORD is the everlasting God, the Creator of the ends of the earth. He does not faint or grow weary; his understanding is unsearchable. He gives power to the faint, and to him who has no might he increases strength. Even youths shall faint and be weary, and young men shall fall exhausted; but they who wait for the LORD shall renew their strength; they shall mount up with wings like eagles; they shall run and not be weary; they shall walk and not faint.

Matthew 11:28-29 ESV Come to me, all who labor and are heavy laden, and I will give you rest. Take my yoke upon you, and learn from me, for I am gentle and lowly in heart, and you will find rest for your souls.

John 3:16 ESV For God so loved the world, that he gave his only Son, that whoever believes in him should not perish but have eternal life.

Psalm 91:14-16 ESV "Because he holds fast to me in love, I will deliver him; I will protect him, because he knows my name. When he calls to me, I will answer him; I will be with him in trouble; I will rescue him and honor him. With long life I will satisfy him and show him my salvation."

Prayers for the Relationships in Your Life

Family Unity

Father I pray that the unity of my family is like that of Colossians 3: ESV: we create and establish an undying harmonic atmosphere. Father we walk and speak in love towards one another. We do not tear down, belittle, or slander one another. My family is on one accord concerning every matter we face with. We have peace which surpasses all understanding, in times of calamity and chaos. My family is a unified praying front that prohibits the infiltration of deceit, division, or animosity. We love one another like Christ loves the church! Father, allow us to be sensitive to the needs of our children and spouse. Let us be able to discern the root of any tense speech or hurt feelings. Let us walk as a unified front in harmony, love, and effective communication. If there is clarity required, may we give it freely without sarcasm or any attitude other than love. I decree that we are conscious of each person's love language, making communication clear and easily accessible between each family member. Father, teach us to confront and rebuke in love when family members may offend us. Teach us to deal with issues according to what your word has commanded of us. Father, we decree that every demonic assignment of outsiders attempting to sow seeds of discord and division in my family has those assignments voided. I plead the blood of Jesus against every generational curse that is set to divide the unity of my family! I declare that my family is one body, individually we do not have the same function but collectively we function as a force that withstands whatever life throws at us! Spirits of pride, haughtiness, arrogance and self-righteousness, you are hereby evicted by the blood of Jesus from ever operating within my family from this day forward. Father you are able to do exceedingly and abundantly above all that we could ever imagine, so I thank you that the burdens of division will never have their place in my family! My family is blessed and all needs are met! My children honor me and as their mother! My spouse loves me like you love the church. All co-parenting relationships (if any) operate under the same unity as one household! I declare that arrogance and judgment will not have any place in my family. We are quick to forgive one another- holding no record of wrong! Unity belongs to my family and nothing or no one can separate us from the love of You or each other.

Scriptures on Family Unity

1 Peter 3:8 ESV Finally, all of you, have unity of mind, sympathy, brotherly love, a tender heart, and a humble mind.

1 Corinthians 1:10 ESV I appeal to you, brothers, by the name of our Lord Jesus Christ, that all of you agree, and that there be no divisions among you, but that you be united in the same mind and the same judgment

Colossians 3:14 ESV And above all these put on love, which binds everything together in perfect harmony.

2 Corinthians 13:11 ESV Finally, brothers, rejoice. Aim for restoration, comfort one another, agree with one another, live in peace; and the God of love and peace will be with you.

Ephesians 4:3 ESV Eager to maintain the unity of the Spirit in the bond of peace.

Romans 12:16 ESV Live in harmony with one another. Do not be haughty, but associate with the lowly. Never be wise in your own sight.

Romans 15:5-7 ESV May the God of endurance and encouragement grant you to live in such harmony with one another, in accord with Christ Jesus, that together you may with one voice glorify the God and Father of our Lord Jesus Christ. Therefore welcome one another as Christ has welcomed you, for the glory of God.

Matthew 18:15 ESV "If your brother sins against you, go and tell him his fault, between you and him alone. If he listens to you, you have gained your brother.

Family Protection

Father from the moment of conception your hand has been upon my life! I decree and declare Psalm 91 which speaks protection over myself and my loved ones in the name of Jesus: A thousand can fall at our sides and ten thousand at our right but it will not come nigh us! You have given your angels charge to keep us in all our ways! No weapon that is formed against me or my family will be able to prosper! Every tongue that rises in judgment will be proven a lie! My family has been redeemed from premature death! We shall live and not die, declaring all the works of The Lord. I rebuke every death assignment against my family with the blood of Jesus! We fulfill every bit of purpose here on earth. We dwell in the secret place of the most high and abide under the shadow of the almighty! You are our refuge and in only you will I trust! I am ever confident that you will deliver me from the snares of the fowler and every noisome pestilence! No evil shall befall my family nor shall any plagues inhabit the places they dwell! You have given your angels charge over me and because of that I rebuke all car accidents, motorcycle accidents, plane mishaps, rape, human trafficking, kidnapping, abuse, and all other violent attacks from off my family and myself in the name of Jesus! God you are our Rock and in you we take refuge! You will deliver us from every oppression and strong hold in the time of trouble! Angels we release you and employ you to go before us warring off any plots, schemes, or strategic destruction the enemy has dispersed to my family! I am thankful Father that You are rebuking the devour on my behalf. Lord you are my ever present help in the time of trouble! My family acknowledges you in all our ways. You are directing our paths! Your word declares that you are faithful and will strengthen and protect us from the evil one! You are neither a man that can lie, nor the son man that can repent. You will perfect every situation that concerns my family! I will not carry the worrying, fear, or burden of my family's protection any longer. My family is blessed and they prosper everyday while present on earth, and will not return to you until your plans established for their lives are completely accomplished.

Scriptures for Family Protection

Job 5:20-21 KJV In famine he will ransom you from death, and in battle from the stroke of the sword. You will be protected from the lash of the tongue, and need not fear when destruction comes.

2 Samuel 22:2-4 KJV "The LORD is my rock, my fortress and my deliverer; my God is my rock, in whom I take refuge, my shield and the horn [a] of my salvation. He is my stronghold, my refuge and my savior— from violent men you save me. I call to the LORD, who is worthy of praise, and I am saved from my enemies."

Psalm 9:9 KJV The LORD is a refuge for the oppressed, a stronghold in times of trouble.

Psalm 12:5 KJV "Because of the oppression of the weak and the groaning of the needy, I will now arise," says the LORD. "I will protect them from those who malign them."

Psalm 18:1-3 KJV I love you, O LORD, my strength. The LORD is my rock, my fortress and my deliverer; my God is my rock, in whom I take refuge. He is my shield and the horn of my salvation, my stronghold. I call to the LORD, who is worthy of praise, and I am saved from my enemies.

Psalm 34:7 KJV The angel of the LORD encamps around those who fear him, and he delivers them.

Psalm121:5-8 KJV The LORD watches over you— the LORD is your shade at your right hand; the sun will not harm you by day, nor the moon by night. The LORD will keep you from all harm— he will watch over your life; the LORD will watch over your coming and going both now and forevermore.

Psalm 138:7 KJV though I walk in the midst of trouble, you preserve my life; you stretch out your hand against the anger of my foes, with your right hand you save me.

Proverbs 3:6 KJV In all thy ways acknowledge him, and he shall direct thy path

Nahum 1:7 KJV The LORD is good, a refuge in times of trouble. He cares for those who trust in him

2 Thessalonians 3:3 KJV The Lord is faithful, and he will strengthen and protect you from the evil one.

Children's Purpose

Father God in Heaven I thank you for finding me worthy enough to loan your children to me while they are here in The Earth. Children are a gift from you and I honor my children as such. God I thank you that at a young age my child has a hunger and thirst for You. God I decree that every seed that you placed inside of them will mature and produce fruit in its season. I declare that my child's purpose will be fulfilled here on earth. I rebuke any scheme or plot that the enemy has assigned to distract, destroy, or deter my child. No weapon that is formed against my child will be able to prosper! I thank you that my child has been redeemed from premature death and freak accidents. I thank you that every place my child's foot treads is blessed! I thank you that the very dreams and passions that you have given them will never be diminished by the negativity of those around them. Lord I thank you that you are surrounding my child with likeminded friends. We cut off all ungodly alliances and sever all ungodly soul ties right now in the name of Jesus. I thank you that as they mature they are not swayed by the customs of this world and only love the things you love. I come against the python spirit that would try to suck out my child's confidence. I call your assignment null and void in the life of my child. My child is assured and unwavering in knowing that they are fearfully and wonderfully made. I thank you that they are good students, athletes, and have a dynamic work ethic. My child is not lazy, slothful or gives in to procrastination. I thank you that they are good stewards over that which you have blessed them with. I thank you in advance that earth is aligning with heaven, producing an atmosphere that is conducive to produce the very resources my child needs to be effective. The words of slander, defeat, statistics, jealousy, bullying and such negativity will not infiltrate the heart, value, or belief system of my child. Lord teach me to comprehend the love language of my child, so that I may be able to effectively communicate my love to them. I declare that when my child hears words from me, they are always coated in patience, love, and encouragement. I will not provoke my child to wrath. I am never swayed or moved in my faith by what my child is involved in! I know that Your hand is upon their life and You are not a God that can fail. I will love and support my child's dream. I will always stand in a posture of expectation; expecting my child to fulfill every bit of purpose as you have set forth in their lives! Sickness, disease and defeat- you will NEVER have my seed! My child is chasing purpose with superior diligence and is destined to accomplish it all!

Scriptures for Children's Purpose

Proverbs 22:6 ESV Train up a child in the way he should go; even when he is old he will not depart from it.

Ephesians 6:4 ESV Fathers, do not provoke your children to anger, but bring them up in the discipline and instruction of the Lord.

Proverbs 13:24 ESV Whoever spares the rod hates his son, but he who loves him is diligent to discipline him.

1 Peter 5:3 ESV Not domineering over those in your charge, but being examples to the flock.

Proverbs 29:17 ESV Discipline your son, and he will give you rest; he will give delight to your heart.

Jeremiah 29:11 ESV For I know the plans I have for you, declares the LORD, plans for welfare and not for evil, to give you a future and a hope.

Romans 8:28 ESV And we know that for those who love God all things work together for good, for those who are called according to his purpose.

Ephesians 2:10 ESV For we are his workmanship, created in Christ Jesus for good works, which God prepared beforehand, that we should walk in them.

Matthew 5:13-15 ESV You are the salt of the earth, but if salt has lost its taste, how shall its saltiness be restored? It is no longer good for anything except to be thrown out and trampled under people's feet. You are the light of the world. A city set on a hill cannot be hidden. Nor do people light a lamp and put it under a basket, but on a stand, and it gives light to all in the house.

Wife

Father God in heaven I thank you for my husband, for I am confident that he is the rib from where my life came from. I thank you father that each day you are teaching me new ways to always maintain the stand of being my husband's 'good thing' that he has found. God in heaven I thank you that even as the two are becoming one that your grace be with us in the transition of facing new situations daily. I thank you that my pride or speech would not be a hindrance in the unification process in our marriage. Father I honor my Husband and the mandate you have called him to. Father I declare that I will always honor and respect him as the head and priest of our household. Father I thank you for the confidence and the assurance that rest in me concerning my husband hearing from you. I am an excellent wife to my husband and I am far more precious than jewels. Father I thank you that I am able to safeguard my husband's vulnerabilities with and level of trust and intimacy that can never be tainted. Father I thank you for exposing every area of division, discord, and contention. I bind up every demonic assignment to divide my marriage right now in the name of Jesus. I only have eyes for my husband and my husband only desires me. I bind the spirit of laziness and slothfulness that tries to attach itself to me during times of sex. Father, allow me to always remember that intimacy with my husband is a form of worship. My husband satisfies me sexually at all times and Father those areas that need improvement give me the words to say that reveal the improvements needed so they are not received in offense. I bind up the spirit of perversion and adultery from my marriage right now in the name of Jesus. Father we are three strand cord, and because we put you first we will never be broken! Father, give me the endurance and discipline to maximize the management of my time between household responsibilities, our children, my career and my husband. Father, train my ear to hear the silent cries of the need of my husband that may come in the form of an argument or heated discussion. Give me the discernment to hear beyond what is said and listen for the root cause. Father I decree and declare that I am not a nag or contentious! Father, teach me to fight my battles correctly in prayer and not in arguments with my husband. I decree and declare that your peace and your love is shed over our marriage in a way neither of us ever knew. I decree and declare that every day I find a new reason to fall in love with my husband! I am confident that I am the strong praying woman my husband needs in order to fulfill purpose! Teach me to strategically pray for my husband and our marriage! This marriage is ordained by God! Will not Fail! We will not Divorce! I am a great wife!

Scriptures on Marriage

Proverbs 18:22 ESV He who finds a wife finds a good thing and obtains favor from the LORD.

Genesis 2:24 ESV Therefore a man shall leave his father and his mother and hold fast to his wife, and they shall become one flesh.

Proverbs 14:1 ESV The wisest of women builds her house, but folly with her own hands tears it down.

Ephesians 5:22 ESV Wives, submit to your own husbands, as to the Lord.
Proverbs 12:4 An excellent wife is the crown of her husband, but she who brings shame is like rottenness in his bones.

Ephesians 5:33 ESV However, let each one of you love his wife as himself, and let the wife see that she respects her husband.

Proverbs 19:14 ESV House and wealth are inherited from fathers, but a prudent wife is from the LORD.

Proverbs 25:24 ESV It is better to live in a corner of the housetop than in a house shared with a quarrelsome wife.

Proverbs 27:15 ESV A continual dripping on a rainy day and a quarrelsome wife are alike.

Single Mothers

Father in every situation you get the glory! You are an intentional God and this very situation is working for my good according to Your word. Even though by worldly standards I appear as a single parent, I know that with You Lord, I never have to parent alone. Your word declares that when our mother and father forsake us you will take us up. Father I decree and declare that regardless of the possible absence of a parent, my child wants for no good thing and all of their needs are met! Father, in You is everything that my child needs to fulfill purpose. I renounce any animosity, bitterness, and the inability for me to forgive my child's father right now in Jesus name. I will continue to let your love and light shine so evidently on my life. I walk in humility and will never act in retaliation because vengeance is yours saith The Lord. I will not be moved in my emotions concerning my child's father or his family. I bind up the spirit of revenge or emotional instability that would cause me to react to situations contrary to the word of God. I decree and declare that nothing will be able to rob me of my peace and power or be able to remove me from a sober minded state. I will not come in between the relationship of my child and their father unless he has the intent to harm my child. Father I decree and declare that my child's father will not be inconsistent and unstable in his presence, but they will be ever present and involved in every stage of growth and development of my child. Father in the name of Jesus I rebuke any demonic influence that would try to attach sprits of abandonment, grief, insecurities or rejection on my child. Father my children have been given the spirit of adoption by which they cry Abba Father. You are their Heavenly father and are fully capable of fulfilling each and every earthly need. I rebuke the identity crisis that would try to connect to my child causing their self-esteem or confidence to waiver. My child is always sure of the fact that he/she is fearfully and wonderfully made. No weapon that is formed against my child would be able to prosper. Father I will not carry the burdens of financial stress, for I will lean on you -my Jehovah Jireh- who is fully able to provide for us. We have food, clothing, and living arrangements that are suitable for the life style I desire. Father I will not use this time alone with my child to remain stagnant, but will constantly work to prepare myself for the rib you created me room. The relationship with my child's earthly father does not define me, nor does hinder me from being fruitful in relationships in the future. I am a great mother. I will consistently instill in my children your word, attributes, and instructions for their life according to Your word.

Scriptures to Help Single Mothers

Philippians 4:13 ESV I can do all things through him who strengthens me.

John 16:33 ESV I have said these things to you, that in me you may have peace. In the world you will have tribulation. But take heart; I have overcome the world."

Ephesians 6:13 ESV Therefore take up the whole armor of God that you may be able to withstand in the evil day, and having done all, to stand firm.

Isaiah 41:13 ESV For I, the LORD your God, hold your right hand; it is I who say to you, "Fear not, I am the one who helps you."

2 Corinthians 10:4 ESV For the weapons of our warfare are not of the flesh but have divine power to destroy strongholds.

Mark 11:24 ESV Therefore I tell you, whatever you ask in prayer, believe that you have received it, and it will be yours.

Deuteronomy 20:4 ESV For the LORD your God is he who goes with you to fight for you against your enemies, to give you the victory.'

Romans 8:28 NIV And we know that in all things God works for the good of those who love him, who have been called according to his purpose.

Romans 12:19 NIV Do not take revenge, my dear friends, but leave room for God's wrath, for it is written: "It is mine to avenge; I will repay," says the Lord.

Ending Ungodly Relationships

Father in the name of Jesus I give you full access to intervene into my life and sever every ungodly relationship, unholy alliance and soul tie. Father I am not persuaded by lust, guilt, loneliness, nor complacency. I decree that my desires line up with the word of God for my life. I declare that I have an unquenchable thirst for your righteousness! Father I end associations with every person in my life that is demonically assigned to distract, stagnate or deter growth and progression in you! I declare that I will not compromise my purpose for the company that I chose to entertain! Father those who are attached to me that are hindering purpose and destiny I asked that you expose and remove them from my life right now in the name of Jesus. Those that you remove I will no longer entertain or allow to creep their way back into my life. I sever the desires of lust and fornication! I renounce the desires to attract approval and attention through lasciviousness behaviors or appearance. I will guard the gates of my soul and not watch or listen to things that cause an arousal of my flesh influencing me to entertain these individuals any longer! I present my body to the world as a living sacrifice holy an acceptable unto You, Oh Lord! Strengthen me in my moments when I want to take my eyes of you and return to filthy ways! I bind of the spirits of Lust, fornication and Jezebel and renounce their operation in my life. My body is filled with the Holy Spirit and all foul and unclean spirits unwelcome. I renounce the desires for sex, masturbation or pornography, as my flesh is under subjection of The Lord. Father I govern every relationship according to 1 Corinthians 13:4—7. I will not play the part of a wife to man that is not my husband gifted and sent by YOU! You have done too much in my life to settle for a relationship that is not ordained by you! I decree that I will not be unequally yoked another day of my life. Father expose every ounce of insecurity that is trying to keep me bound in the relationship connected to sin! I harken my ears to hear what you are saying concerning this relationship and the voice of the stranger that man I will not follow. I will not tolerate anyone treating me contrary to the way you treat your bride- the church! I love You and myself too much and today this relationship will rule me NO longer!

Scriptures on Ending Ungodly Relationships

1 Corinthians 13:4-7 ESV Love is patient and kind; love does not envy or boast; it is not arrogant or rude. It does not insist on its own way; it is not irritable or resentful; it does not rejoice at wrongdoing, but rejoices with the truth. Love bears all things, believes all things, hopes all things, endures all things

Galatians 5:19-21 ESV Now the works of the flesh are evident: sexual immorality, impurity, sensuality, idolatry, sorcery, enmity, strife, jealousy, fits of anger, rivalries, dissensions, divisions, envy, drunkenness, orgies, and things like these. I warn you, as I warned you before, that those who do such things will not inherit the kingdom of God

Romans 12:1-2 ESV I appeal to you therefore, brothers, by the mercies of God, to present your bodies as a living sacrifice, holy and acceptable to God, which is your spiritual worship. Do not be conformed to this world, but be transformed by the renewal of your mind, that by testing you may discern what is the will of God, what is good and acceptable and perfect.

1 Corinthians 6:18 ESV Flee from sexual immorality. Every other sin a person commits is outside the body, but the sexually immoral person sins against his own body.

2 Corinthians 6:14 ESV Do not be unequally yoked with unbelievers. For what partnership has righteousness with lawlessness? Or what fellowship has light with darkness?

Matthew 5:27-28 ESV "You have heard that it was said, 'You shall not commit adultery.' But I say to you that everyone who looks at a woman with lustful intent has already committed adultery with her in his heart.

Post Breakup/Separation Prayer

Father no matter who walks in or out of my life you God are forever with me. My comforter! My strong tower that I can run into and be safe! My friend that sticks closer than a brother! My help! My all in all! Your word declares that you stick close to the brokenhearted, so I know right now you are close and wrapping me in your arms renewing my strength. Father I thank you in my times of weakness you are reaching down into the depths of my heart and mending the broken pieces. I thank you that you are restoring my joy even in the midst of tears! You are my rock! God you make no mistakes and in you there is no failure! This is not a setback in my life, but this is separation is for a next level elevation. I thank you Lord that I am coming out of this place stronger, wiser, and better prepared for my purpose in the earth! I thank you that this pain is temporary but the growth from this place is eternal! I will lift up my head in spite of the heaviness of my heart! I will make it through this! He that has begun a good work in me shall surely bring it to pass! I am stronger than this current state! This is not a defining moment, but a refining moment! I come out of this place pure gold! I declare that in this broken place I will not seek refuge in temporary hobbies, companion, or indulgences that deceive me into an altered reality. I stand firm in seeking refuge in only you and your word! I am who God says I am! Fearfully wonderfully made! God is refining me into become the wife I need to be for the husband he has for me! Sanctify my mind, appearance and intentions Father! Create in me a clean heart and renew the right and acceptable spirit with in me. I declare that my lifestyle and desires are holy and righteous from this day forward. I place my flesh under subjection to the Holy Spirit! Weeping may endure for a night but joy comes in the morning, right now at this very moment- THIS IS MORNING! My joy is returning right now as I decree and declare it in the mightily name of Jesus! I believe, there for I speak! Joy is mine! Peace is mine! Wisdom and understanding is mine! I thank you that in this season you are preparing me for the husband you created me for! I will never return to this place of hurt another day in my life!

Scriptures Post Breakup/Separation

Revelation 21:4 ESV "He will wipe away every tear from their eyes, and death shall be no more, neither shall there be mourning, nor crying, nor pain anymore, for the former things have passed away."

John 14:27 ESV "Peace I leave with you; my peace I give to you. Not as the world gives do I give to you. Let not your hearts be troubled, neither let them be afraid.

Isaiah 41:10 ESV "Fear not, for I am with you; be not dismayed, for I am your God; I will strengthen you, I will help you, I will uphold you with my righteous right hand."

Matthew 11:28-30 ESV "Come to me, all who labor and are heavy laden, and I will give you rest. Take my yoke upon you, and learn from me, for I am gentle and lowly in heart, and you will find rest for your souls. For my yoke is easy, and my burden is light."

Deuteronomy 31:6 ESV "Be strong and courageous. Do not be afraid or terrified because of them, for the Lord your God goes with you; he will never leave you nor forsake you."

Philippians 4:13 ESV "I can do all things through Him who gives me strength

Prayers for Abundant Living

Prosperity

Father God in the name of Jesus, I thank you that you have given me all things that pertain to life and godliness. I thank you Lord that you are my great shepherd and in You I have no lack! Right now as I pray, Angels are warring on my behalf to return unto me all the wealth that has been demonically bound in my bloodline! I curse every tactic that the enemy is using to block up my increase right now! The python spirit is broken off of my finances right now in the name of Jesus. Father you are not a man that can lie, nor the son of man that must repent! As you have commanded I have honored you with my tithe and offering as my commitment and faith in you as the Financier of my life. I meditate on the words of Mark 6:31-32, and they are a reality of my life! As I give unto You, I rest in knowing you have people assigned already to give back unto me! Favor, Goodness and Mercy are hotly pursuing me all the days of my life. The tailored made blessings you have for me are running me down right now in the name of Jesus. I get into covenant agreement with the words of 2 Corinthians 9:8. I am living my life in abundance. As according to Philippians 4:9, you are the supplier of all my needs. All manner of lack in my life are cut off at the root. I prophesy the blessings of Abraham and favor of Joseph over my life. Every place that my feet shall tread is blessed! I am blessed coming in and blessed going out! No weapon that is strategically assigned to choke my increase will be able to prosper! I am blessed and the blessings of Godly prosperity run through my bloodline. My children's children, and their children will partake of the seal of prosperity over my life. I curse every habit in me which is linked to the mentality of a poor man! As your word states, "above all else you desire that we PROSPER and be in health even as our soul's prosper!" You delight in the prosperity of Your servant. As You delight in my increase, I will continue to delight myself in your word. According to Joshua 1:8, I meditate on your word day and night; my mediations are making my way prosperous and creating my success. I decree and declare that I am a homeowner-mortgage is paid on time and in full! I rebuke the customs of interest in the system of this world in all things. I am the lender and not the borrower. I am a good steward of which thou has blessed me with! I will not beg, borrow, or covet! Spirit of laziness and slothfulness I curse you at the root! I decree and declare that I will seize every opportunity of increase that you have granted unto me! BLESSED! I AM BLESSED IN EVERY ASPECT OF MY LIFE- ESPECIALLY IN MY FINANCES!

Scriptures for Prosperity

Philippians 4:19 ESV And my God will supply every need of yours according to his riches in glory in Christ Jesus.

Deuteronomy 8:18 ESV You shall remember the LORD your God, for it is he who gives you power to get wealth, that he may confirm his covenant that he swore to your fathers, as it is this day.

Psalm 128:2 ESV You shall eat the fruit of the labor of your hands; you shall be blessed, and it shall be well with you.

2 Corinthians 9:8 ESV And God is able to make all grace abound to you, so that having all sufficiency in all things at all times, you may abound in every good work.

Joshua 1:9 ESV Have I not commanded you? Be strong and courageous. Do not be frightened, and do not be dismayed, for the LORD your God is with you wherever you go."

Psalm 1:3 ESV He is like a tree planted by streams of water that yields its fruit in its season, and its leaf does not wither. In all that he does, he prospers.

Luke 6:38 ESV Give, and it will be given to you. Good measure, pressed down, shaken together, running over, will be put into your lap. For with the measure you use it will be measured back to you."

Jeremiah 29:11-14 ESV For I know the plans I have for you, declares the LORD, plans for welfare and not for evil, to give you a future and a hope. Then you will call upon me and come and pray to me, and I will hear you. You will seek me and find me, when you seek me with all your heart. I will be found by you, declares the LORD, and I will restore your fortunes and gather you from all the nations and all the places where I have driven you, declares the LORD, and I will bring you back to the place from which I sent you into exile.

Psalm 34:8-10 ESV Oh, taste and see that the LORD is good! Blessed is the man who takes refuge in him! Oh, fear the LORD, you his saints, for those who fear him have no lack! The young lions suffer want and hunger; but those who seek the LORD lack no good thing.

Deuteronomy 28:12 ESV The LORD will open to you his good treasury, the heavens, to give the rain to your land in its season and to bless all the work of your hands. And you shall lend to many nations, but you shall not borrow.

Proverbs 10:22 ESV The blessing of the LORD makes rich, and he adds no sorrow with it.

Matthew 6:33 ESV But seek first the kingdom of God and his righteousness, and all these things will be added to you.

Debt Cancelation

Father debt is a form of bondage and in your word you declare that Your desire for my life that I prosper and be in health even as my soul prosper. Your word declares that if I seek first the kingdom of God and your righteousness all things will be added unto me. Father I take dominion over my debt and declare that in Jesus name I am out of debt, all needs being met right now in Jesus name. Father I decree and declare that mortgages, car loans, business loans, bank loans, student loans, and medical bills are paid in full right now in the name of Jesus. Father, it is You that gives us power to attain wealth. I thank you right now as you are revealing unto me areas in which I can seize every door of opportunity open unto me for financial increase. Father I thank you for a miracle right now in my financial situation. I declare that I am a good steward over that which you have blessed me with! I am a tither and I believe for your financial favor in every situation like I have never seen before! You are raising up individuals to give unto my bosom a good measure pressed down shaken together and running over! Policies and rules are being changed on my behalf interest payments, principle amounts, and late fees are being cancelled right now in Jesus name. I speak to this mountain of debt and declare that you be removed right now in the name of Jesus! Loose your hold right now! I am the seed of Abraham which the Lord has blessed. Your word promises me that that you will supply all of my needs according to your riches in glory by Christ Jesus. Satan I bind up your activity in my finances and debt right now in Jesus name. Ministering spirits of God go forth securing all the funds that are needed for me to have surplus in my deliverance from debt. From this day forward my accounts will never be in the red! I will not live pay check to pay check! I will pay my tithes! My outstanding balances are paid in full in Jesus name!

Scriptures on Debt Cancellation

Philippians 4:19 ESV And my God will supply every need of yours according to his riches in glory in Christ Jesus.

Malachi 3:10 ESV Bring the full tithe into the storehouse, that there may be food in my house. And thereby put me to the test, says the LORD of hosts, if I will not open the windows of heaven for you and pour down for you a blessing until there is no more need

3 John 1:2 ESV Beloved, I pray that all may go well with you and that you may be in good health, as it goes well with your soul.

Psalm 128:2 ESV You shall eat the fruit of the labor of your hands; you shall be blessed, and it shall be well with you

2 Corinthians 9:8 ESV And God is able to make all grace abound to you, so that having all sufficiency in all things at all times, you may abound in every good work.

Psalm 1:3 ESV He is like a tree planted by streams of water that yields its fruit in its season, and its leaf does not wither. In all that he does, he prospers.

2 Corinthians 8:9 ESV For you know the grace of our Lord Jesus Christ, that though he was rich, yet for your sake he became poor, so that you by his poverty might become rich.

Luke 6:38 ESV Give, and it will be given to you. Good measure, pressed down, shaken together, running over, will be put into your lap. For with the measure you use it will be measured back to you."

Psalm 34:8-10 ESV Oh, taste and see that the LORD is good! Blessed is the man who takes refuge in him! Oh, fear the LORD, you his saints, for those who fear him have no lack! The young lions suffer want and hunger; but those who seek the LORD lack no good thing.

Deuteronomy 28:12 ESV The LORD will open to you his good treasury, the heavens, to give the rain to your land in its season and to bless all the work of your hands. And you shall lend to many nations, but you shall not borrow.

Entrepreneur Woman

Your word declares that I can do all things through Christ that strengthens me! Your word declares that greater is He that is in me than he that is in the world! God I thank you that the boldness and confidence I had when I stepped out on faith to start my business follows me all the days of my life. I thank you that daily my profit, network, and net worth are increasing exponentially! Your favor hotly pursues me in every meeting, client interaction, and negotiations with lenders. I thank you for a debt free business that is blessed to be a blessing to others! I thank you that I am a good steward over that which you have abundantly blessed me with. I thank you for provision and witty ideas concerning marketing strategy and business growth and development. I thank you for providing a plan and the resources to have dominion over untapped and supersaturated markets! This is the business You mandated me to birth, therefore I am in competition with no other business. For Your favor rests mightily on my business and we prosper in every situation. I thank you Lord for the proper employees under me to help launch this business into the next dimension You have for it. Lord I thank you for sending legal support to ensure that my company is protected in structure, laws, patents, copyrights and trademarks. I thank you Lord for a great public relations officer, social media marketer, accountant, and advisor that fear you and will do right by this business in execution of vision and in growth. I thank you for new loyal contracts and clientele that are greatly satisfied with the services provided. Procrastination, slothfulness, and complacency are never a part of my business work ethic! I am a well-balanced entrepreneur that efficiently manages time, supersedes my goals, and surpass expectations for myself and my business. Lord develop in me a dynamic leader that possesses all the character traits are required to take this business to the heights You have destined for it. I seize every opportunity for advancement under Your direction. I may be the boss, but Lord you are the CEO. I will never make any decisions without consulting You. Train my ear to hear from you concerning my business like never before! I thank you for raising up people, partners and philanthropists to sow seeds into my business! The company will never be in lack will prosper in every aspect! Fear, doubt, and lack of faith, you are under my feet in the name of Jesus! Recession and economic setbacks are never attached to my business. God is the CEO of this business and in him there is no failure!

Scriptures for Entrepreneurs

Deuteronomy 8:18 NIV But remember the LORD your God, for it is he who gives you the ability to produce wealth, and so confirms his covenant, which he swore to your ancestors, as it is today.

Peter 4:10 NIV Each of you should use whatever gift you have received to serve others, as faithful stewards of God's grace in its various forms

Corinthians 13:5-6 NIV Examine yourselves to see whether you are in the faith; test yourselves. Do you not realize that Christ Jesus is in you--unless, of course, you fail the test? And I trust that you will discover that we have not failed the test.

Isaiah 45:2 NIV I will go before you and will level the mountains; I will break down gates of bronze and cut through bars of iron

Mark 5:36 NIV Overhearing what they said, Jesus told them, "Don't be afraid; just believe."

Peter 5:8 NIV Be alert and of sober mind. Your enemy the devil prowls around like a roaring lion looking for someone to devour.

Proverbs 2:6-8 NIV For the LORD gives wisdom; from his mouth come knowledge and understanding. He holds success in store for the upright, he is a shield to those whose walk is blameless, for he guards the course of the just and protects the way of his faithful ones

Ephesians 6:12 NIV For our struggle is not against flesh and blood, but against the rulers, against the authorities, against the powers of this dark world and against the spiritual forces of evil in the heavenly realms Philippians 3:13-14 NIV Brothers and sisters, I do not consider myself yet to have taken hold of it. But one thing I do: Forgetting what is behind and straining toward what is ahead, I press on toward the goal to win the prize for which God has called me heavenward in Christ Jesus.

Joshua 1:9 NIV Have I not commanded you? Be strong and courageous. Do not be terrified; do not be discouraged, for the LORD your God will be with you wherever you go.

Atmosphere at Work

Father your word declares that I am blessed in the city and blessed in the field! Wherever my feet shall tread will be called blessed! I thank you that as I travel to my place of employment. Right now as I pray, the climate of my job is shifting in my favor! I decree and declare that nothing of a negative nature will be able to shift the climate which I establish while at work. I forbid any attacks, slander, lies, or confusion from attaching themselves to my name, position, or the work I produce! I thank you that I have favor with the company CEO, direct supervisor, and all those you place over me. I thank you Lord that promotion comes from you and not from my human abilities! I will not force my way into a position that is not in your will for me. I thank you that I will not be easily distracted by negativity, gossip, and unproductive employees! My systems and equipment will work properly without setbacks or glitches so that I can perform the work that is expected of me. I will be a good steward over time management today, and give my job the time that they are paying me for. I love my job for the very reason that God is cultivating the character, patience, and wisdom I need for promotion. I thank you Lord that you have blessed me with a resource to provide for myself and my family. I will never lose sight of the fact that you, God alone, are my source. I thank you that I am properly recognized and awarded for the diligent and error free work produced. I meet all deadlines and supersede all goals set for myself pertaining to my job and career. Father I make a conscious decision that even in difficult and intense situations I respond with tact and the joy of the Lord. Satan will get no victory out of my actions at work today and all of my days there. I am not easily frustrated or irritated and will not be moved in my emotions. I will not fear my work load; for your word declares that I can do all things through Christ who strengthens me, and I am a workforce overcomer. I will operate in humility and patience at all times! I will maintain a godly countenance. I will always keep my eyes and attitude on the focus of why God has me here. I will be a light amongst my coworkers and I will not be afraid to share with them who you are to me. I thank you Lord for opening up doors of opportunity to witness to my coworkers. I thank you in advance that I will boldly seize every opportunity to spread your love and light on my job! I will win today on my job! All things pertaining to this job are working for my God! I am happy today and of good cheer, and declare nothing will change my mood concerning my job!

Scriptures on Atmosphere at Work

Colossians 3:23 ESV Whatever you do, work heartily, as for the Lord and not for men.

Proverbs 16:3 ESV Commit your work to the LORD, and your plans will be established.

Proverbs 10:4 ESV A slack hand causes poverty, but the hand of the diligent makes rich.

Acts 20:35 ESV In all things I have shown you that by working hard in this way we must help the weak and remember the words of the Lord Jesus, how he himself said, 'It is more blessed to give than to receive.'

1 Corinthians 10:31 ESV So, whether you eat or drink, or whatever you do, do all to the glory of God.

1 Timothy 5:8 ESV But if anyone does not provide for his relatives, and especially for members of his household, he has denied the faith and is worse than an unbeliever.

Matthew 5:16 ESV In the same way, let your light shine before others, so that they may see your good works and give glory to your Father who is in heaven.
Ephesians 4:28 ESV Let the thief no longer steal, but rather let him labor, doing honest work with his own

hands, so that he may have something to share with anyone in need.

Proverbs 20:4 ESV The sluggard does not plow in the autumn; he will seek at harvest and have nothing.

Proverbs 20:13 ESV Love not sleep, lest you come to poverty; open your eyes, and you will have plenty of bread.

Psalm 1:1-6 ESV Blessed is the man who walks not in the counsel of the wicked, nor stands in the way of sinners, nor sits in the seat of scoffers; but his delight is in the law of the LORD, and on his law he meditates day and night. He is like a tree planted by streams of water that yields its fruit in its season, and its leaf does not wither. In all that he does, he prospers. The wicked are not so, but are like chaff that the wind drives away. Therefore the wicked will not stand in the judgment, nor sinners in the congregation of the righteous...

Purchaser's Prayer

Father God in heaven before I make the decision to make this purchase this item I declare that your wisdom, knowledge, and understanding be given unto me freely and unhindered. I lay aside my anxious desires to move without hearing clearly from you! Father, go before me and secure the best financial arrangement for me saturated with favor. Father, expose any plots, schemes, and hidden agendas to wrongfully take advantage of me and misappropriation of my money right now in the name of Jesus. Discernment you be enhanced right now in Jesus name! I will not move until you say so God. I will not be anxious due to deadlines for you Father, are the author of time. I declare that I am not moved in my emotions when I am told no or not approved. Father with you all things are possible! Angels I release and assign you to go forth and secure that what is mine and reveal to me that which is the tailored made blessing for me. Father, remove any smoke screens that would deceive me into purchasing the wrong item! I decree and declare that I hear clearly the direction of God. I have favor in every situation. Rules, policies and prices are changing on my behalf to accommodate me in the financial state God has me in. I adjourn the schemes of over priced items, elevated interest rates, hidden fees and unfavorable contracts right now in the name of Jesus. Father I declare that I will trust in you with all my heart and lean not into my own understanding concerning this purchase. Father close every door that is not a tailored made blessing for me. I decree and declare that I will not be in debt or upside down in my finances after this purchase! This purchase is not a setback; for you are increasing me daily. Money you increase right now in the name of Jesus! Wealth and riches are my God given right and they belong to me in Jesus name. This purchase will increase and add to my family- without adding sorrow! For your word declares Your blessings only make me rich! Father, speak now like only you can! I won't move until I hear clearly from you! Favor go before me and secure that which God has for me in the mighty and excellent name of Jesus.

Scriptures for when making a purchase

James 1:5 ESV If any of you lacks wisdom, let him ask God, who gives generously to all without reproach, and it will be given him.

Proverbs 3:5 ESV Trust in the LORD with all your heart, and do not lean on your own understanding.

Mark 11:24 ESV Therefore I tell you, whatever you ask in prayer, believe that you have received it, and it will be yours.

Philippians 4:6 ESV Do not be anxious about anything, but in everything by prayer and supplication with thanksgiving let your requests be made known to God.

Matthew 6:31-33 ESV Therefore do not be anxious, saying, 'What shall we eat?' or 'What shall we drink?' or 'What shall we wear?' For the Gentiles seek after all these things, and your heavenly Father knows that you need them all. But seek first the kingdom of God and his righteousness, and all these things will be added to you.

Philippians 4:19 ESV And my God will supply every need of yours according to his riches in glory in Christ Jesus.

Proverbs 8:18 ESV Riches and honor are with me, enduring wealth and righteousness.

Deuteronomy 28:11 ESV And the LORD will make you abound in prosperity, in the fruit of your womb and in the fruit of your livestock and in the fruit of your ground, within the land that the LORD swore to your fathers to give you.

Psalm 112:3 ESV Wealth and riches are in his house, and his righteousness endures forever

2 Corinthians 9:6 ESV The point is this: whoever sows sparingly will also reap sparingly, and whoever sows bountifully will also reap bountifully.

Training Your Mouth to Speak God's Language

New Language

Remove those curse words from your vocabulary that are not your typical 4 Letter words. Often times we don't even realize that the subconscious words and slogans we speak have a habit of saying cancel our prayers. These words are often said habitually without much thought given. In order to receive the things requested in prayer, we need to learn a new vernacular or culture of speech. We need to rid our conversations of vocabulary which attributes to death, doubt, lack of faith, and unbelief; regardless of self-talk or speaking among others. The bible declares that blessing and cursing should not come from the same lips. In the same manner why should we declare healing and sickness out of the same mouth? When your speech begins to line up with the word of God; your words are then backed by the unchanging word of God. My challenge to you is from this day forward rid your communications of these death producing sayings, and watch your entire life change for the better. You will start to see the very things you ask for manifest quickly in your life. Some examples of common sayings that you should remove from your vocabulary are listed below. Begin to examine your speech. Examine the negative statements. Begin to write them on the blank pages provided, so they too can be removed from your speech immediately. As you write, think of the substitutes of positivity and life you can replace the statements with.

Note: This list is not inclusive, and should be tailored for personal use.

"I'm sick and tired…"

"I can't…"

"I'm dying/died laughing"

"I'm dead"

"I'll never get out of debt"

"I'll never get over this"

"It's impossible…"

"It won't work…"

"I can't stand…"

"I give up…"

"He/She kills me"

"I'll never be able to…"

"You're getting/working on my nerves.."

"My diabetes, high blood pressure, cholesterol, etc"

(NEVER take ownership of sickness, Healing BELONGS to you!)

"Oh my God"

"I can't with her/him"

"I can't handle this…"

"I give up"

"I love you to death"

"I hate…"

"It's killing me…"

"I'm struggling"

About the Author

Meagan Farrare is 28 year old preacher, teacher, author, and dynamic prayer warrior. She has been serving God whole heartedly since the age of 14. Meagan received her formal education from Delaware Public School System and upon graduating she attended Valley Forge Christian College majoring in Pastoral Ministry. During her first year in college, Meagan started traveling to various place to preach to include Arkansas, Arizona, New York and the DMV area. At the age of 19 while still in school, Meagan enlisted into the world's greatest air power the Delaware Air National Guard and she continues to serve her nation and state to this day.

In the year of 2015 God directed Meagan to start Women of Purpose a ministry to empower women through the principles of Sisterhood, Prayer, and Community Outreach. In the one year of their existence Women of Purpose also launched Men of Purpose that is under the direction of her husband Terrance Farrare. As well as mentoring program for girl's ages 12-17 named God's Purposed Girls, GPG is a program that deals with goal planning, self-esteem, and abstaining until marriage.

Meagan is blessed to be the wife of Terrance Farrare and mother to an amazing daughter named Autumn. Meagan has boldly accepted the call on her life and greatly honored that God would use her as a vessel to stir up the gifts inside of those she encounters launching them toward fulfilling every bit of purpose God has called them to.

For booking information email:
BookingMFarrare@gmail.com

40596081R00066

Made in the USA
Middletown, DE
17 February 2017